D0572212

CLASSIC RECIPES™

Publications International, Ltd.

Favorite Brand Name Recipes at www.fbnr.com

Copyright © 2003 Publications International, Ltd.
Recipes and text copyright © 2003 Eagle Family Foods, Inc.
All rights reserved. This publication may not be reproduced or quoted in whole or in part
by any means whatsoever without written permission from:

Louis Weber, CEO
Publications International, Ltd.
7373 North Cicero Avenue
Lincolnwood, IL 60712

Permission is never granted for commercial purposes.

Classic Recipes is a trademark of Publications International, Ltd.

Borden and Elsie are trademarks used under license from BDH Two, Inc. © 2003
Eagle Family Foods, Inc.

Illustration by Kathrin Goldman.

Pictured on the front cover: Double Delicious Cookie Bars *(page 32)*.

ISBN: 1-4127-2337-X

Manufactured in China.

8 7 6 5 4 3 2 1

Microwave Cooking: Microwave ovens vary in wattage. Use the cooking times as
guidelines and check for doneness before adding more time.

Preparation/Cooking Times: Preparation times are based on the approximate amount
of time required to assemble the recipe before cooking, baking, chilling or serving. These
times include preparation steps such as measuring, chopping and mixing. The fact that
some preparations and cooking can be done simultaneously is taken into account.
Preparation of optional ingredients and serving suggestions is not included.

Table of Contents

Fabulous Bars

Who can resist Magic Cookie Bars? No one can! This is just one of the Eagle® Brand classics that has been loved by families for generations.

Magic Cookie Bars

   $^1/_2$ cup (1 stick) butter or margarine
 1$^1/_2$ cups graham cracker crumbs
   1 (14-ounce) can EAGLE® BRAND Sweetened Condensed Milk
        (NOT evaporated milk)
   2 cups (12 ounces) semi-sweet chocolate chips
 1$^1/_3$ cups flaked coconut
   1 cup chopped nuts

1. Preheat oven to 350°F (325°F for glass dish). In 13×9-inch baking pan, melt butter in oven.

2. Sprinkle crumbs over butter; pour Eagle Brand evenly over crumbs. Layer evenly with remaining ingredients; press down firmly.

3. Bake 25 minutes or until lightly browned. Cool. Chill, if desired. Cut into bars. Store loosely covered at room temperature.

Makes 2 to 3 dozen bars

Prep Time: 10 minutes
Bake Time: 25 minutes

7-Layer Magic Cookie Bars: Substitute 1 cup (6 ounces) butterscotch-flavored chips* for 1 cup semi-sweet chocolate chips.

* Peanut butter-flavored chips or white chips may be substituted for butterscotch-flavored chips.

Magic Peanut Cookie Bars: Substitute 2 cups (about $^3/_4$ pound) chocolate-covered peanuts for semi-sweet chocolate chips and chopped nuts.

Magic Rainbow Cookie Bars: Substitute 2 cups plain candy-coated chocolate pieces for semi-sweet chocolate chips.

Double Chocolate Fantasy Bars

1 (18.25-ounce) package chocolate cake mix

¼ cup vegetable oil

1 egg

1 cup chopped nuts

1 (14-ounce) can EAGLE® BRAND Sweetened Condensed Milk
     (NOT evaporated milk)

1 (6-ounce) package semi-sweet chocolate chips

1 teaspoon vanilla extract

Dash salt

1. Preheat oven to 350°F. Grease 13×9-inch baking pan. In large mixing bowl, combine cake mix, oil and egg; beat at medium speed until crumbly. Stir in nuts. Reserve 1½ cups crumb mixture. Press remaining crumb mixture on bottom of prepared pan.

2. In small saucepan over medium heat, combine remaining ingredients. Cook and stir until chips melt.

3. Pour chocolate mixture evenly over prepared crust. Sprinkle reserved crumb mixture evenly over top. Bake 25 to 30 minutes or until set. Cool. Cut into bars. Store loosely covered at room temperature.

Makes about 3 dozen bars

Prep Time: 15 minutes
Bake Time: 25 to 30 minutes

Top to bottom: Double Chocolate Fantasy Bars and Toffee Bars (page 19)

Chewy Almond Squares

1 1/4 cups graham cracker crumbs

1/3 cup (2/3 stick) butter or margarine, melted

1/4 cup sugar

1 cup flaked coconut, toasted

1 cup chopped almonds, toasted*

1 (14-ounce) can EAGLE® BRAND Sweetened Condensed Milk
(NOT evaporated milk)

*1 cup chopped pecans or walnuts, toasted, may be substituted.

1. Preheat oven to 375°F. Line 9-inch square pan with foil. In medium mixing bowl, combine crumbs, butter and sugar. Press into bottom of prepared pan. Bake 5 to 7 minutes.

2. Sprinkle crust with coconut and almonds; pour Eagle Brand evenly over surface.

3. Bake 25 to 30 minutes. Cool on wire rack. Cut into squares. Store covered at room temperature.   *Makes 16 squares*

Prep Time: 10 minutes
Bake Time: 30 to 37 minutes

Top to bottom: Chewy Almond Squares and Marbled Cheesecake Bars (page 12)

Marbled Cheesecake Bars

2 cups finely crushed crème-filled chocolate sandwich cookie
   crumbs (about 24 cookies)

3 tablespoons butter or margarine, melted

3 (8-ounce) packages cream cheese, softened

1 (14-ounce) can EAGLE® BRAND Sweetened Condensed Milk
   (NOT evaporated milk)

3 eggs

2 teaspoons vanilla extract

2 (1-ounce) squares unsweetened chocolate, melted

1. Preheat oven to 300°F. Line 13×9-inch baking pan with heavy foil; set aside. Combine crumbs and butter; press firmly on bottom of prepared pan.

2. In large mixing bowl, beat cream cheese until fluffy. Gradually beat in Eagle Brand until smooth. Add eggs and vanilla; mix well. Pour half the batter evenly over prepared crust.

3. Stir melted chocolate into remaining batter; spoon over vanilla batter. With table knife or metal spatula, gently swirl through batter to marble.

4. Bake 45 to 50 minutes or until set. Cool. Chill. Cut into bars. Store covered in refrigerator. *Makes 2 to 3 dozen bars*

Prep Time: 20 minutes
Bake Time: 45 to 50 minutes

Helpful Hint: For even marbling, do not oversoften or overbeat the cream cheese.

Brownie Mint Sundae Squares

1 (21.5- or 23.6-ounce) package fudge brownie mix

³/4 cup coarsely chopped walnuts

1 (14-ounce) can EAGLE® BRAND Sweetened Condensed Milk (NOT evaporated milk)

2 teaspoons peppermint extract

Green food coloring, if desired

2 cups (1 pint) whipping cream, whipped

¹/2 cup mini chocolate chips

Chocolate ice cream topping, if desired

1. Line 13×9-inch baking pan with aluminum foil; grease foil. Prepare brownie mix as package directs; stir in walnuts. Spread in prepared pan. Bake as directed. Cool completely.

2. In large mixing bowl, combine Eagle Brand, peppermint extract and food coloring, if desired. Fold in whipped cream and chips. Pour over brownie layer; cover.

3. Freeze 6 hours or until firm. To serve, lift brownies from pan with foil; cut into squares. Serve with chocolate ice cream topping, if desired. Freeze leftovers. *Makes 12 servings*

Cheesecake-Topped Brownies

1 (21.5- or 23.6-ounce) package fudge brownie mix

1 (8-ounce) package cream cheese, softened

2 tablespoons butter or margarine, softened

1 tablespoon cornstarch

1 (14-ounce) can EAGLE® BRAND Sweetened Condensed Milk
   (NOT evaporated milk)

1 egg

2 teaspoons vanilla extract

   Ready-to-spread chocolate frosting, if desired

   Orange peel, if desired

1. Preheat oven to 350°F. Prepare brownie mix as package directs.
Spread into well-greased 13×9-inch baking pan.

2. In large mixing bowl, beat cream cheese, butter and cornstarch until
fluffy.

3. Gradually beat in Eagle Brand. Add egg and vanilla; beat until smooth.
Pour cheesecake mixture evenly over brownie batter.

4. Bake 40 to 45 minutes or until top is lightly browned. Cool. Spread
with frosting or sprinkle with orange peel, if desired. Cut into bars. Store
covered in refrigerator.   *Makes 3 to 3 1/2 dozen brownies*

Prep Time: 20 minutes
Bake Time: 40 to 45 minutes

Cheesecake-Topped Brownies

Chocolate Nut Bars

1³/₄ cups graham cracker crumbs

¹/₂ cup (1 stick) butter or margarine, melted

1 (14-ounce) can EAGLE® BRAND Sweetened Condensed Milk (NOT evaporated milk)

2 cups (12 ounces) semi-sweet chocolate chips, divided

1 teaspoon vanilla extract

1 cup chopped nuts

1. Preheat oven to 375°F. Combine crumbs and butter; press firmly on bottom of 13×9-inch baking pan. Bake 8 minutes. Reduce oven temperature to 350°F.

2. In small saucepan over medium heat, melt Eagle Brand with 1 cup chocolate chips and vanilla. Spread chocolate mixture over prepared crust. Top with remaining 1 cup chocolate chips, then nuts; press down firmly.

3. Bake 25 to 30 minutes. Cool. Chill if desired. Cut into bars. Store loosely covered at room temperature.   *Makes 2 to 3 dozen bars*

Prep Time: 10 minutes
Bake Time: 33 to 38 minutes

Chocolate Nut Bars

Lemony Cheesecake Bars

1 1/2 cups graham cracker crumbs
1/3 cup sugar
1/3 cup finely chopped pecans
1/3 cup butter or margarine, melted
2 (8-ounce) packages cream cheese, softened
1 (14-ounce) can EAGLE® BRAND Sweetened Condensed Milk
   (NOT evaporated milk)
2 eggs
1/2 cup lemon juice from concentrate

1. Preheat oven to 325°F. In medium mixing bowl, combine crumbs, sugar, pecans and melted butter. Reserve 1/3 cup crumb mixture; press remaining mixture into 13×9-inch baking pan. Bake 5 minutes. Remove from oven and cool on wire rack.

2. In large mixing bowl, beat cream cheese until fluffy. Gradually beat in Eagle Brand until smooth. Add eggs; beat until just combined. Stir in lemon juice. Carefully spoon mixture onto crust in pan. Spoon reserved crumb mixture to make diagonal stripes on top of cheese mixture or sprinkle to cover.

3. Bake about 30 minutes or until knife inserted near center comes out clean. Cool on wire rack 1 hour. Cut into bars to serve. Store in refrigerator. *Makes 3 dozen bars*

Prep Time: 25 minutes
Bake Time: 35 minutes

Toffee Bars

1 cup quick-cooking oats
$^1/_2$ cup all-purpose flour
$^1/_2$ cup firmly packed light brown sugar
$^1/_2$ cup finely chopped walnuts
$^1/_2$ cup (1 stick) butter or margarine, melted and divided
$^1/_4$ teaspoon baking soda
1 (14-ounce) can EAGLE® BRAND Sweetened Condensed Milk
    (NOT evaporated milk)
2 teaspoons vanilla extract
2 cups (12 ounces) semi-sweet chocolate chips
    Additional chopped walnuts, if desired

1. Preheat oven to 350°F. Grease 13×9-inch baking pan. In large mixing bowl, combine oats, flour, brown sugar, walnuts, 6 tablespoons butter and baking soda. Press firmly on bottom of prepared pan. Bake 10 to 15 minutes or until lightly browned.

2. Meanwhile, in medium saucepan over medium heat, combine remaining 2 tablespoons butter and Eagle Brand. Cook and stir until mixture thickens slightly, about 15 minutes. Remove from heat; stir in vanilla. Pour evenly over baked crust.

3. Bake 10 to 15 minutes or until golden brown.

4. Remove from oven; immediately sprinkle chips on top. Let stand 1 minute; spread chips while still warm. Garnish with additional walnuts, if desired; press down firmly. Cool completely. Cut into bars. Store tightly covered at room temperature.   *Makes 3 dozen bars*

Lemon Crumb Bars

1 (18.25-ounce) package lemon or yellow cake mix

$^1/_2$ cup (1 stick) butter or margarine, softened

1 egg

2 cups finely crushed saltine cracker crumbs

3 egg yolks

1 (14-ounce) can EAGLE® BRAND Sweetened Condensed Milk
     (NOT evaporated milk)

$^1/_2$ cup lemon juice from concentrate

1. Preheat oven to 350°F. Grease 15×10-inch jelly-roll pan. In large mixing bowl, combine cake mix, butter and 1 egg; mix well (mixture will be crumbly). Stir in cracker crumbs. Reserve 2 cups crumb mixture. Press remaining crumb mixture firmly on bottom of prepared pan. Bake 15 minutes.

2. Meanwhile, in medium mixing bowl, combine egg yolks, Eagle Brand and lemon juice; mix well. Spread evenly over baked crust.

3. Top with reserved crumb mixture. Bake 20 minutes or until firm. Cool. Cut into bars. Store covered in refrigerator.   *Makes 3 to 4 dozen bars*

Prep Time: 30 minutes
Bake Time: 35 minutes

Lemon Crumb Bars

Toffee-Top Cheesecake Bars

1 ¼ cups all-purpose flour

1 cup powdered sugar

½ cup unsweetened cocoa

¼ teaspoon baking soda

¾ cup (1 ½ sticks) butter or margarine

1 (8-ounce) package cream cheese, softened

1 (14-ounce) can EAGLE® BRAND Sweetened Condensed Milk
(NOT evaporated milk)

2 eggs

1 teaspoon vanilla extract

1 ½ cups (8-ounce package) English toffee bits, divided

1. Preheat oven 350°F. In medium mixing bowl, combine flour, powdered sugar, cocoa and baking soda; cut in butter until mixture is crumbly. Press into bottom of ungreased 13×9-inch baking pan. Bake 15 minutes.

2. Beat cream cheese until fluffy. Add Eagle Brand, eggs and vanilla; beat until smooth. Stir in 1 cup English toffee bits. Pour mixture over hot crust. Bake 25 minutes or until set and edges just begin to brown.

3. Remove from oven. Cool 15 minutes. Sprinkle remaining ½ cup English toffee bits evenly over top. Cool completely. Refrigerate several hours or until cold. Store leftovers covered in refrigerator.

Makes about 3 dozen bars

Prep Time: 20 minutes
Bake Time: 40 minutes
Cool Time: 15 minutes

Toffee-Top Cheesecake Bars

German Chocolate Cheesecake Bars

1 1/2 cups graham cracker crumbs

1/2 cup sugar

1/2 cup butter or margarine, melted

3 (8-ounce) packages cream cheese, softened

1 (14-ounce) can EAGLE® BRAND Sweetened Condensed Milk (NOT evaporated milk)

2 (4-ounce) packages semi-sweet chocolate, melted

3 eggs

1 tablespoon vanilla extract

Coconut Pecan Topping (recipe follows)

1. Preheat oven to 350°F. In medium mixing bowl, combine crumbs, sugar and butter; press on bottom of 15×10-inch jelly-roll pan. In large mixing bowl, beat cream cheese until fluffy. Gradually beat in Eagle Brand until smooth. Add remaining ingredients except topping; mix well. Pour over crust.

2. Bake 20 minutes or until center is set. Cool. Top with Coconut Pecan Topping. Chill. Cut into bars. Refrigerate leftovers.

Makes 3 to 4 dozen bars

Coconut Pecan Topping

1 (14-ounce) can EAGLE® BRAND Sweetened Condensed Milk (NOT evaporated milk)

3 egg yolks

1/2 cup butter or margarine

1 1/3 cups flaked coconut

1 cup chopped pecans

1 teaspoon vanilla extract

1. In heavy saucepan, combine Eagle Brand and egg yolks; mix well. Add butter. Over medium-low heat, cook and stir until thickened and bubbly, 8 to 10 minutes.

2. Remove saucepan from heat; stir in coconut, pecans and vanilla. Cool 10 minutes. *Makes about 2¾ cups*

Frozen Lemon Squares

1¼ cups graham cracker crumbs

¼ cup sugar

¼ cup (½ stick) butter or margarine, melted

1 (14-ounce) can EAGLE® BRAND Sweetened Condensed Milk (NOT evaporated milk)

3 egg yolks

½ cup lemon juice from concentrate

Yellow food coloring, if desired

Whipped cream or non-dairy whipped topping

1. Preheat oven to 325°F. Combine crumbs, sugar and butter; press firmly on bottom of 8- or 9-inch square pan.

2. In medium mixing bowl, beat Eagle Brand, egg yolks, lemon juice and food coloring, if desired. Pour into crust.

3. Bake 30 minutes. Cool completely. Top with whipped cream. Freeze 4 hours or until firm. Let stand 10 minutes before serving. Garnish as desired. Freeze leftovers. *Makes 6 to 9 squares*

Fudge-Filled Bars

1 (14-ounce) can EAGLE® BRAND Sweetened Condensed Milk
    (NOT evaporated milk)
1 (12-ounce) package semi-sweet chocolate chips
2 tablespoons butter or margarine
2 teaspoons vanilla extract
2 (18-ounce) packages refrigerated cookie dough (oatmeal-
    chocolate chip, chocolate chip, or sugar cookie dough),
    divided

1. Preheat oven to 350°F. In heavy saucepan over medium heat, combine Eagle Brand, chips and butter; heat until chips melt, stirring often. Remove from heat; stir in vanilla. Cool 15 minutes.

2. Using floured hands, press 1½ packages of cookie dough into ungreased 15×10-inch jelly-roll pan. Pour cooled chocolate mixture evenly over dough. Crumble remaining dough over chocolate mixture.

3. Bake 25 to 30 minutes. Cool. Cut into bars. Store covered at room temperature.   *Makes 4 dozen bars*

Prep Time: 20 minutes
Bake Time: 25 to 30 minutes

Helpful Hint: If you want to trim the fat in any Eagle Brand recipe, just use Eagle® Brand Fat Free or Low Fat Sweetened Condensed Milk instead of the original Eagle Brand.

Fudge-Filled Bars

No-Bake Fudgy Brownies

1 (14-ounce) can EAGLE® BRAND Sweetened Condensed Milk
    (NOT evaporated milk)
2 (1-ounce) squares unsweetened chocolate, cut up
1 teaspoon vanilla extract
2 cups plus 2 tablespoons packaged chocolate cookie crumbs,
    divided
$1/4$ cup miniature candy-coated milk chocolate candies or chopped
    nuts

1. Grease 8-inch square baking pan or line with foil; set aside.

2. In medium-sized heavy saucepan, combine Eagle Brand and chocolate; cook and stir over low heat just until boiling. Reduce heat; cook and stir for 2 to 3 minutes more or until mixture thickens. Remove from heat. Stir in vanilla.

3. Stir in 2 cups cookie crumbs. Spread evenly in prepared pan. Sprinkle with remaining cookie crumbs and candies or nuts; press down gently with back of spoon.

4. Cover and chill 4 hours or until firm. Cut into squares. Store covered in refrigerator.   *Makes 2 to 3 dozen brownies*

Prep Time: 10 minutes
Chill Time: 4 hours

No-Bake Fudgy Brownies

Buckeye Cookie Bars

1 (18.25-ounce) package chocolate cake mix

$^1/_4$ cup vegetable oil

1 egg

1 cup chopped peanuts

1 (14-ounce) can EAGLE® BRAND Sweetened Condensed Milk
   (NOT evaporated milk)

$^1/_2$ cup peanut butter

1. Preheat oven to 350°F. In large mixing bowl, combine cake mix, oil and egg; beat at medium speed until crumbly. Stir in peanuts. Reserve 1$^1/_2$ cups crumb mixture; press remaining crumb mixture firmly on bottom of greased 13×9 inch baking pan.

2. In medium mixing bowl, beat Eagle Brand with peanut butter until smooth; spread over prepared crust. Sprinkle with reserved crumb mixture.

3. Bake 25 to 30 minutes or until set. Cool. Cut into bars. Store loosely covered at room temperature.   *Makes 2 to 3 dozen bars*

Prep Time: 20 minutes
Bake Time: 25 to 30 minutes

Double Chocolate Brownies

1 1/4 cups all-purpose flour, divided

1/4 cup sugar

1/2 cup (1 stick) cold butter or margarine

1 (14-ounce) can EAGLE® BRAND Sweetened Condensed Milk
     (NOT evaporated milk)

1/4 cup unsweetened cocoa

1 egg

1 teaspoon vanilla extract

1/2 teaspoon baking powder

1 (8-ounce) milk chocolate bar, broken into chunks

3/4 cup chopped nuts, if desired

1. Preheat oven to 350°F. Line 13×9-inch baking pan with foil; set aside.

2. In medium mixing bowl, combine 1 cup flour and sugar; cut in butter until crumbly. Press firmly on bottom of prepared pan. Bake 15 minutes.

3. In large mixing bowl, beat Eagle Brand, cocoa, egg, remaining 1/4 cup flour, vanilla and baking powder. Stir in chocolate chunks and nuts, if desired. Spread over baked crust. Bake 20 minutes or until set.

4. Cool. Use foil to lift out of pan. Cut into bars. Store tightly covered at room temperature.   *Makes 2 dozen brownies*

Prep Time: 15 minutes
Bake Time: 35 minutes

Double Delicious Cookie Bars

$^{1}/_{2}$ cup (1 stick) butter or margarine

1$^{1}/_{2}$ cups graham cracker crumbs

1 (14-ounce) can EAGLE® BRAND Sweetened Condensed Milk
(NOT evaporated milk)

2 cups (12 ounces) semi-sweet chocolate chips*

1 cup (6 ounces) peanut butter-flavored chips*

*Butterscotch-flavored chips or white chocolate chips can be substituted for the semi-sweet chocolate chips and/or peanut butter-flavored chips.

1. Preheat oven to 350°F (325°F for glass dish). In 13×9-inch baking pan, melt butter in oven.

2. Sprinkle crumbs evenly over butter; pour Eagle Brand evenly over crumbs. Top with remaining ingredients; press down firmly.

3. Bake 25 to 30 minutes or until lightly browned. Cool. Cut into bars. Store covered at room temperature.   *Makes 2 to 3 dozen bars*

Prep Time: 10 minutes
Bake Time: 25 to 30 minutes

Double Delicious Cookie Bars

Golden Peanut Butter Bars

2 cups all-purpose flour

$^3/_4$ cup firmly packed light brown sugar

1 egg, beaten

$^1/_2$ cup (1 stick) cold butter or margarine

1 cup finely chopped peanuts

1 (14-ounce) can EAGLE® BRAND Sweetened Condensed Milk
(NOT evaporated milk)

$^1/_2$ cup peanut butter

1 teaspoon vanilla extract

1. Preheat oven to 350°F. In large mixing bowl, combine flour, brown sugar and egg; cut in cold butter until crumbly. Stir in peanuts. Reserve 2 cups crumb mixture. Press remaining mixture on bottom of 13×9-inch baking pan.

2. Bake 15 minutes or until lightly browned.

3. Meanwhile, in another large mixing bowl, beat Eagle Brand, peanut butter and vanilla. Spread over prepared crust; top with reserved crumb mixture.

4. Bake an additional 25 minutes or until lightly browned. Cool. Cut into bars. Store covered at room temperature.   *Makes 2 to 3 dozen bars*

Prep Time: 20 minutes
Bake Time: 40 minutes

Golden Peanut Butter Bars

Sensational Cookies

Fill your cookie jar with scrumptious treats. You can whip up these cookies in minutes and watch them disappear quicker than a wink!

Chocolate Peanut Butter Chip Cookies

8 (1-ounce) squares semi-sweet chocolate

3 tablespoons butter or margarine

1 (14-ounce) can EAGLE® BRAND Sweetened Condensed Milk (NOT evaporated milk)

2 cups biscuit baking mix

1 egg

1 teaspoon vanilla extract

1 cup (6 ounces) peanut butter-flavored chips

1. Preheat oven to 350°F. In large saucepan over low heat, melt chocolate and butter with Eagle Brand; remove from heat. Add biscuit mix, egg and vanilla; with mixer, beat until smooth and well blended.

2. Let mixture cool to room temperature. Stir in peanut butter chips. Shape into 1¼-inch balls. Place 2 inches apart on ungreased baking sheets. Bake 6 to 8 minutes or until tops are lightly crusty. Cool. Store tightly covered at room temperature.   *Makes about 4 dozen cookies*

Prep Time: 15 minutes
Bake Time: 6 to 8 minutes

Double Chocolate Cherry Cookies

1¼ cups (2½ sticks) butter or margarine, softened

1¾ cups sugar

2 eggs

1 tablespoon vanilla extract

3½ cups all-purpose flour

¾ cup unsweetened cocoa

½ teaspoon baking powder

½ teaspoon baking soda

¼ teaspoon salt

2 (6-ounce) jars maraschino cherries, well drained and halved (about 60 cherries)

1 (6-ounce) package semi-sweet chocolate chips

1 (14-ounce) can EAGLE® BRAND Sweetened Condensed Milk (NOT evaporated milk)

1. Preheat oven to 350°F. In large mixing bowl, beat butter and sugar until fluffy. Add eggs and vanilla; mix well.

2. In large mixing bowl, combine dry ingredients; stir into butter mixture (dough will be stiff). Shape into 1-inch balls. Place 1 inch apart on ungreased baking sheets. Press cherry half into center of each cookie. Bake 8 to 10 minutes. Cool.

3. In heavy saucepan over medium heat, melt chips with Eagle Brand; cook until mixture thickens, about 3 minutes. Frost each cookie, covering cherry. Store loosely covered at room temperature.

Makes about 10 dozen cookies

Prep Time: 25 minutes

Bake Time: 8 to 10 minutes

Double Chocolate Pecan Cookies: Prepare and shape dough as directed above, omitting cherries. Flatten. Bake and frost as directed. Garnish each cookie with pecan half.

Coconut Macaroons

1 (14-ounce) can EAGLE® BRAND Sweetened Condensed Milk (NOT evaporated milk)
2 teaspoons vanilla extract
1 to $1^1/_2$ teaspoons almond extract
2 (7-ounce) packages flaked coconut ($5^1/_3$ cups)

1. Preheat oven to 325°F. Line baking sheets with foil; grease and flour foil. Set aside.

2. In large mixing bowl, combine Eagle Brand, vanilla and almond extract. Stir in coconut. Drop by rounded teaspoonfuls onto prepared sheets; with spoon, slightly flatten each mound.

3. Bake 15 to 17 minutes or until golden. Remove from baking sheets; cool on wire racks. Store loosely covered at room temperature.

Makes about 4 dozen cookies

Prep Time: 10 minutes
Bake Time: 15 to 17 minutes

Chocolate Chip Treasure Cookies

1½ cups graham cracker crumbs
½ cup all-purpose flour
2 teaspoons baking powder
1 (14-ounce) can EAGLE® BRAND Sweetened Condensed Milk
    (NOT evaporated milk)
½ cup (1 stick) butter or margarine, softened
1⅓ cups flaked coconut
1 (12-ounce) package semi-sweet chocolate chips
1 cup chopped walnuts

1. Preheat oven to 375°F. In small mixing bowl, combine crumbs, flour and baking powder.

2. In large mixing bowl, beat Eagle Brand and butter until smooth. Add crumb mixture; mix well. Stir in coconut, chips and walnuts.

3. Drop by rounded tablespoonfuls onto ungreased cookie sheets. Bake 9 to 10 minutes or until lightly browned. Store loosely covered at room temperature.   *Makes about 3 dozen cookies*

Prep Time: 15 minutes
Bake Time: 9 to 10 minutes

Clockwise from top: Chocolate Chip Treasure Cookies, Cookies 'n' Crème Fudge (page 74), Double Chocolate Brownie (page 31) and Magic Cookie Bar (page 7)

Magic Make It Your Way Drop Cookies

    3 cups sifted all-purpose flour
    3 teaspoons baking powder
    ³⁄₄ teaspoon salt
    ³⁄₄ cup (1¹⁄₂ sticks) butter or margarine, softened
    2 eggs
    1 teaspoon vanilla extract
    1 (14-ounce) can EAGLE® BRAND Sweetened Condensed Milk
        (NOT evaporated milk)
    One "favorite" ingredient (see below)

1. Preheat oven to 350°F. Grease baking sheets; set aside. In large mixing bowl, sift together dry ingredients. Stir in butter, eggs, vanilla and Eagle Brand. Fold in one of your "favorite" ingredients.

2. Drop by level teaspoonfuls, about 2 inches apart, onto prepared baking sheets. Bake 8 to 10 minutes or until edges are slightly browned. Remove at once from baking sheet. Cool. Store covered at room temperature.

Makes about 4 dozen cookies

"Make it your way" with your favorite ingredient (pick one):
1 (6-ounce) package semi-sweet chocolate chips
1¹⁄₂ cups raisins
1¹⁄₂ cups corn flakes
1¹⁄₂ cups toasted shredded coconut

Prep Time: 15 minutes
Bake Time: 8 to 10 minutes

No-Bake Peanutty Chocolate Drops

$^1/_2$ cup (1 stick) butter or margarine

$^1/_3$ cup unsweetened cocoa

2$^1/_2$ cups quick-cooking oats

1 (14-ounce) can EAGLE® BRAND Sweetened Condensed Milk
    (NOT evaporated milk)

1 cup chopped peanuts

$^1/_2$ cup peanut butter

1. Line baking sheets with waxed paper. In medium saucepan over medium heat, melt butter; stir in cocoa. Bring mixture to a boil.

2. Remove from heat; stir in remaining ingredients.

3. Drop by teaspoonfuls onto prepared baking sheets; chill 2 hours or until set. Store loosely covered in refrigerator.

Makes about 5 dozen drops

Prep Time: 10 minutes
Chill Time: 2 hours

Double Chocolate Cookies

2 cups biscuit baking mix

1 (14-ounce) can EAGLE® BRAND Sweetened Condensed Milk
(NOT evaporated milk)

8 (1-ounce) squares semi-sweet chocolate *or* 1 (12-ounce) package
semi-sweet chocolate chips, melted

3 tablespoons butter or margarine, melted

1 egg

1 teaspoon vanilla extract

6 (1¼-ounce) white chocolate candy bars with almonds, broken
into small pieces

¾ cup chopped nuts

1. Preheat oven to 350°F. In large mixing bowl, combine all ingredients except candy pieces and nuts; beat until smooth.

2. Stir in remaining ingredients. Drop by rounded teaspoonfuls, 2 inches apart, onto ungreased baking sheets.

3. Bake 10 minutes or until tops are slightly crusted (do not overbake). Cool. Store tightly covered at room temperature.

Makes about 4½ dozen cookies

Prep Time: 15 minutes
Bake Time: 10 minutes

Mint Chocolate Cookies: Substitute ¾ cup mint-flavored chocolate chips for white chocolate candy bars with almonds. Proceed as directed above.

Top to bottom: Double Chocolate Cookies and Chocolate Raspberry Truffles (page 75)

Macaroon Kisses

1 (14-ounce) can EAGLE® BRAND Sweetened Condensed Milk
(NOT evaporated milk)
2 teaspoons vanilla extract
1 to 1½ teaspoons almond extract
5⅓ cups (14 ounces) flaked coconut
48 solid milk chocolate candy kisses, stars or drops, unwrapped

1. Preheat oven to 325°F. Line baking sheets with foil; grease and flour foil. Set aside.

2. In large mixing bowl, combine Eagle Brand, vanilla and almond extract. Stir in coconut. Drop by rounded teaspoonfuls onto foil-lined sheets; slightly flatten each mound with spoon.

3. Bake 15 to 17 minutes or until golden brown. Remove from oven. Immediately press candy kiss, star or drop in center of each macaroon. Remove from baking sheets; cool on wire racks. Store loosely covered at room temperature.   *Makes 4 dozen cookies*

To measure Eagle Brand easily, remove the entire lid first, and then scrape the Eagle Brand into a glass measuring cup using a rubber scraper.

Macaroon Kisses

Easy Peanut Butter Cookies

1 (14-ounce) can EAGLE® BRAND Sweetened Condensed Milk
(NOT evaporated milk)
3/4 to 1 cup peanut butter
1 egg
1 teaspoon vanilla extract
2 cups biscuit baking mix
Sugar

1. In large mixing bowl, beat Eagle Brand, peanut butter, egg and vanilla until smooth. Add biscuit mix; mix well. Chill at least 1 hour.

2. Preheat oven to 350°F. Shape dough into 1-inch balls. Roll in sugar. Place 2 inches apart on ungreased baking sheets.

3. Flatten with fork in criss-cross pattern. Bake 6 to 8 minutes or until lightly browned (do not overbake). Cool. Store tightly covered at room temperature. *Makes about 5 dozen cookies*

Prep Time: 10 minutes
Chill Time: 1 hour
Bake Time: 6 to 8 minutes

Peanut Butter & Jelly Gems: Make dough as directed above. Shape into 1-inch balls and roll in sugar; do not flatten. Press thumb in center of each ball of dough; fill with jelly, jam or preserves. Proceed as directed above.

Any-Way-You-Like 'em Cookies: Stir 1 cup semi-sweet chocolate chips, chopped peanuts, raisins or flaked coconut into dough. Proceed as directed above.

Peanut Blossom Cookies

1 (14-ounce) can EAGLE® BRAND Sweetened Condensed Milk
(NOT evaporated milk)
3/4 cup peanut butter
2 cups biscuit mix
1 teaspoon vanilla extract
1/3 cup sugar
60 solid milk chocolate candy kisses, unwrapped

1. Preheat oven to 375°F. In large mixing bowl, beat Eagle Brand and peanut butter until smooth. Add biscuit mix and vanilla; mix well. Shape into 1-inch balls. Roll in sugar. Place 2-inches apart on ungreased baking sheets.

2. Bake 6 to 8 minutes or until lightly browned (do not overbake). Immediately remove from oven; press candy kiss in center of each cookie. Cool. Store tightly covered at room temperature.

Makes about 5 dozen cookies

Cookies and desserts made with Eagle Brand contain condensed all-natural milk. This gives your family important bone-building calcium in every bite.

Luscious Cakes & More

Make any day a celebration with these delightful cakes, cheesecakes and other sweet treats. You'll find they are fun to make—and impossible to resist.

Cherry-Topped Lemon Cheesecake Pie

1 (8-ounce) package cream cheese, softened

1 (14-ounce) can EAGLE® BRAND Sweetened Condensed Milk
    (NOT evaporated milk)

$^1/_3$ cup lemon juice from concentrate

1 teaspoon vanilla extract

1 (6-ounce) ready-made graham cracker crumb pie crust

1 (21-ounce) can cherry pie filling, chilled

1. In large mixing bowl, beat cream cheese until fluffy. Gradually beat in Eagle Brand until smooth. Stir in lemon juice and vanilla. Pour into crust. Chill at least 3 hours.

2. To serve, top with cherry pie filling. Store covered in refrigerator.

Makes 6 to 8 servings

Prep Time: 10 minutes

Chill Time: 3 hours

For a firmer crust, brush crust with slightly beaten
egg white; bake in 375°F oven 5 minutes. Cool
before pouring filling into crust.

Raspberry Swirl Cheesecakes

$1^1/_2$ cups fresh or thawed lightly sweetened loose-pack frozen red
    raspberries
1 (14-ounce) can EAGLE® BRAND Sweetened Condensed Milk
    (NOT evaporated milk), divided
2 (8-ounce) packages cream cheese, softened
3 eggs
2 (6-ounce) chocolate-flavored crumb pie crusts
    Chocolate and white chocolate leaves (recipe follows), if desired
    Fresh raspberries, if desired

1. Preheat oven to 350°F. In blender container, blend $1^1/_2$ cups
raspberries until smooth; press through sieve to remove seeds. Stir $^1/_3$ cup
Eagle Brand into sieved raspberries; set aside.

2. In large mixing bowl, beat cream cheese, eggs and remaining Eagle
Brand. Spoon into crusts. Drizzle with raspberry mixture. With table
knife, gently swirl raspberry mixture through cream cheese mixture.

3. Bake 25 minutes or until center is nearly set when shaken. Cool; chill
at least 4 hours. Garnish with chocolate leaves and fresh raspberries, if
desired. Store leftovers covered in refrigerator.

Makes 16 servings (2 cheesecakes)

Prep Time: 15 minutes
Bake Time: 25 minutes
Chill Time: 4 hours

Chocolate Leaves: Place 1 (1-ounce) square semi-sweet or white chocolate in microwave-safe bowl. Microwave at HIGH (100% power) 1 to 2 minutes, stirring every minute until smooth. With small, clean paintbrush, paint several coats of melted chocolate on the undersides of nontoxic leaves, such as mint, lemon or strawberry. Wipe off any chocolate from top sides of leaves. Place leaves, chocolate sides up, on waxed paper-lined baking sheet or on curved surface, such as rolling pin. Refrigerate leaves until chocolate is firm. To use, carefully peel leaves away from chocolate.

Rich Caramel Cake

    1 (14-ounce) package caramels, unwrapped
    ½ cup (1 stick) butter or margarine
    1 (14-ounce) can EAGLE® BRAND Sweetened Condensed Milk
        (NOT evaporated milk)
    1 (18.25 or 18.5-ounce) package chocolate cake mix
    1 cup coarsely chopped pecans

1. Preheat oven 350°F. In heavy saucepan over low heat, melt caramels and butter. Remove from heat; add Eagle Brand. Mix well. Set aside caramel mixture. Prepare cake mix as package directs.

2. Spread 2 cups cake batter into greased 13×9-inch baking pan; bake 15 minutes. Spread caramel mixture evenly over cake; spread remaining cake batter over caramel mixture. Top with pecans. Return to oven; bake 30 to 35 minutes or until cake springs back when lightly touched. Cool.

Makes 10 to 12 servings

Triple Chocolate Cheesecakes

1 envelope unflavored gelatin

1/2 cup cold water

2 (8-ounce) packages cream cheese, softened

1 (14-ounce) can EAGLE® BRAND Sweetened Condensed Milk (NOT evaporated milk)

4 (1-ounce) squares unsweetened chocolate, melted and slightly cooled

1 (8-ounce) carton frozen non-dairy whipped topping, thawed

1/2 cup (3 ounces) mini semi-sweet chocolate chips

1 (21-ounce) can cherry pie filling, if desired

2 (6-ounce) ready-made chocolate crumb pie crusts

1. In 1-cup glass measure, stir together gelatin and cold water; let stand 5 minutes to soften. Pour about 1 inch water into small saucepan; place glass measure in saucepan. Place saucepan over medium heat; stir until gelatin is dissolved. Remove measure from saucepan; cool slightly.

2. In large mixing bowl, combine cream cheese, Eagle Brand and melted chocolate; beat until smooth. Gradually beat in gelatin mixture. Fold in whipped topping and chips.

3. Spread pie filling on bottoms of crusts, if desired. Spoon chocolate mixture into pie crusts. Cover and chill at least 4 hours. Store covered in refrigerator.   *Makes 12 servings (2 cheesecakes)*

Prep Time: 20 minutes
Chill Time: 4 hours

Triple Chocolate Cheesecake

Black Forest Chocolate Cheesecake

1 1/2 cups chocolate cookie or wafer crumbs

3 tablespoons butter or margarine, melted

2 (1-ounce) squares unsweetened chocolate

1 (14-ounce) can EAGLE® BRAND Sweetened Condensed Milk
(NOT evaporated milk)

2 (8-ounce) packages cream cheese, softened

3 eggs

3 tablespoons cornstarch

1 teaspoon almond extract

1 (21-ounce) can cherry pie filling, chilled

1. Preheat oven to 300°F. Combine cookie crumbs with butter; press firmly on bottom of 9-inch springform pan.

2. In small saucepan over low heat, melt chocolate with Eagle Brand, stirring constantly. Remove from heat.

3. In large mixing bowl, beat cream cheese until fluffy. Gradually add Eagle Brand mixture until smooth. Add eggs, cornstarch and almond extract; mix well. Pour into crust.

4. Bake 55 minutes or until center is almost set. Cool. Chill. Top with cherry pie filling before serving. Refrigerate leftovers.

Makes one 9-inch cheesecake

Microwave Cheesecake

$^1/_3$ cup ($^2/_3$ stick) butter or margarine

1$^1/_4$ cups graham cracker crumbs

$^1/_4$ cup sugar

2 (8-ounce) packages cream cheese, softened

1 (14-ounce) can EAGLE® BRAND Sweetened Condensed Milk
(NOT evaporated milk)

3 eggs

$^1/_4$ cup lemon juice from concentrate

1 (8-ounce) container sour cream, at room temperature

1. In 10-inch microwave-safe quiche dish or pie plate, melt butter loosely covered at HIGH (100% power) 1 minute. Add crumbs and sugar; press firmly on bottom of dish. Microwave at HIGH (100% power) 1$^1/_2$ minutes, rotating dish once.

2. In 2-quart glass measure, beat cream cheese until fluffy. Gradually beat in Eagle Brand until smooth. Add eggs and lemon juice; mix well. Microwave at MEDIUM-HIGH (70% power) 6 to 8 minutes or until hot, stirring every 2 minutes.

3. Pour into prepared crust. Microwave at MEDIUM (50% power) 6 to 8 minutes or until center is set, rotating dish once. Top with sour cream. Cool. Chill 3 hours or until set. Serve or top with fruit, if desired. Store covered in refrigerator. *Makes one 10-inch cheesecake*

Prep Time: 15 minutes
Cook Time: 14$^1/_2$ to 18$^1/_2$ minutes
Chill Time: 3 hours

Fudge Ribbon Cake

1 (18.25-ounce) package chocolate cake mix

1 (8-ounce) package cream cheese, softened

2 tablespoons butter or margarine, softened

1 tablespoon cornstarch

1 (14-ounce) can EAGLE® BRAND Sweetened Condensed Milk
(NOT evaporated milk)

1 egg

1 teaspoon vanilla extract

Chocolate Glaze (recipe follows)

1. Preheat oven to 350°F. Grease and flour 13×9-inch baking pan. Prepare cake mix as package directs. Pour batter into prepared pan.

2. In small mixing bowl, beat cream cheese, butter and cornstarch until fluffy. Gradually beat in Eagle Brand. Add egg and vanilla; beat until smooth. Spoon evenly over cake batter.

3. Bake 40 minutes or until wooden pick inserted near center comes out clean. Cool. Prepare Chocolate Glaze and drizzle over cake. Store covered in refrigerator. *Makes 10 to 12 servings*

Prep Time: 20 minutes
Bake Time: 40 minutes

Chocolate Glaze: In small saucepan over low heat, melt 1 (1-ounce) square unsweetened or semi-sweet chocolate and 1 tablespoon butter or margarine with 2 tablespoons water. Remove from heat. Stir in $3/4$ cup powdered sugar and $1/2$ teaspoon vanilla extract. Stir until smooth and well blended. Makes about $1/3$ cup.

Fudge Ribbon Bundt Cake: Preheat oven to 350°F. Grease and flour 10-inch Bundt pan. Prepare cake mix as package directs. Pour batter into prepared pan. Prepare cream cheese topping as directed above; spoon evenly over batter. Bake 50 to 55 minutes or until wooden pick inserted near center comes out clean. Cool 10 minutes. Remove from pan. Cool. Prepare Chocolate Glaze and drizzle over cake. Store covered in refrigerator.

Fudge Ribbon Cake

Lemon Party Cheesecake

1 (18.25- or 18.5-ounce) package yellow cake mix*
4 eggs, divided
$^1/_4$ cup vegetable oil*
2 (8-ounce) packages cream cheese, softened
1 (14-ounce) can EAGLE® BRAND Sweetened Condensed Milk
(NOT evaporated milk)
$^1/_4$ to $^1/_3$ cup lemon juice from concentrate
2 teaspoons grated lemon peel, if desired
1 teaspoon vanilla extract

If "pudding added" cake mix is used, decrease oil to 3 tablespoons.

1. Preheat oven to 300°F. Reserve $^1/_2$ cup dry cake mix. In large mixing bowl, combine remaining cake mix, 1 egg and oil; mix well (mixture will be crumbly). Press down firmly on bottom and $1^1/_2$ inches up sides of greased 13×9-inch baking pan.

2. In same bowl, beat cream cheese until fluffy. Gradually beat in Eagle Brand until smooth. Add remaining 3 eggs and reserved $^1/_2$ cup cake mix; beat on medium speed 1 minute. Stir in lemon juice, lemon peel, if desired, and vanilla.

3. Pour into crust. Bake 50 to 55 minutes or until center is set. Cool to room temperature. Chill thoroughly. Cut into squares to serve. Garnish as desired. Refrigerate leftovers.   *Makes 12 to 15 servings*

Prep Time: 20 minutes
Bake Time: 55 minutes

Cool and Minty Party Cake

1 (14-ounce) can EAGLE® BRAND Sweetened Condensed Milk
(NOT evaporated milk)

2 teaspoons peppermint extract

8 drops green food coloring, if desired

2 cups (1 pint) whipping cream, whipped (do not use non-dairy
topping)

1 (18.25- or 18.5-ounce) package white cake mix
Green crème de menthe liqueur

1 (8-ounce) container frozen non-dairy whipped topping, thawed

1. Line 9-inch round layer cake pan with aluminum foil. In large mixing
bowl, combine Eagle Brand, peppermint extract and food coloring, if
desired. Fold in whipped cream. Pour into prepared pan; cover. Freeze at
least 6 hours or until firm.

2. Meanwhile, prepare and bake cake mix as package directs for two 9-inch
round layers. Remove from pans; cool completely.

3. With fork, poke holes in cake layers 1-inch apart halfway through each
layer. Spoon small amounts of liqueur in holes. Place one cake layer on
serving plate; top with ice cream layer, then second cake layer. Trim ice
cream layer to edge of cake layers.

4. Frost quickly with whipped topping. Return to freezer at least 6 hours
before serving. Garnish as desired. Freeze leftovers.

Makes one 9-inch cake

Creamy Baked Cheesecake

1$^1/_4$ cups graham cracker crumbs

$^1/_4$ cup sugar

$^1/_3$ cup ($^2/_3$ stick) butter or margarine, melted

2 (8-ounce) packages cream cheese, softened

1 (14-ounce) can EAGLE® BRAND Sweetened Condensed Milk (NOT evaporated milk)

3 eggs

$^1/_4$ cup lemon juice from concentrate

1 (8-ounce) container sour cream, at room temperature

Raspberry Topping (recipe follows), if desired

1. Preheat oven to 300°F. In small mixing bowl, combine crumbs, sugar and butter; press firmly on bottom of ungreased 9-inch springform pan.

2. In large mixing bowl, beat cream cheese until fluffy. Gradually beat in Eagle Brand until smooth. Add eggs and lemon juice; mix well. Pour into prepared pan. Bake 50 to 55 minutes or until set.

3. Remove from oven; top with sour cream. Bake 5 minutes longer. Cool. Chill. Prepare Raspberry Topping, if desired, and serve with cheesecake. Store covered in refrigerator. *Makes one 9-inch cheesecake*

Prep Time: 20 minutes

Bake Time: 55 to 60 minutes

Chill Time: 4 hours

New York Style Cheesecake: Increase cream cheese to 4 (8-ounce) packages and eggs to 4. Proceed as directed, adding 2 tablespoons flour after eggs. Bake 1 hour 10 minutes or until center is set. Omit sour cream. Cool. Chill. Serve and store as directed.

Raspberry Topping

1 (10-ounce) package thawed frozen red raspberries in syrup
$1/4$ cup red currant jelly or red raspberry jam
1 tablespoon cornstarch

1. Drain $2/3$ cup syrup from raspberries.

2. In small saucepan over medium heat, combine syrup, jelly and cornstarch. Cook and stir until slightly thickened and clear. Cool. Stir in raspberries.

Prep Time: 5 minutes

Creamy Baked Cheesecake

Chocolate Sheet Cake

1 1/4 cups (2 1/2 sticks) butter or margarine, divided

1 cup water

1/2 cup unsweetened cocoa, divided

2 cups all-purpose flour

1 1/2 cups firmly packed light brown sugar

1 teaspoon baking soda

1 teaspoon ground cinnamon

1/2 teaspoon salt

1 (14-ounce) can EAGLE® BRAND Sweetened Condensed Milk (NOT evaporated milk), divided

2 eggs

1 teaspoon vanilla extract

1 cup powdered sugar

1 cup coarsely chopped nuts

1. Preheat oven to 350°F. In small saucepan over medium heat, melt 1 cup butter; stir in water and 1/4 cup cocoa. Bring to a boil; remove from heat. In large mixing bowl, combine flour, brown sugar, baking soda, cinnamon and salt. Add cocoa mixture; beat well. Stir in 1/3 cup Eagle Brand, eggs and vanilla. Pour into greased 15×10-inch jelly-roll pan. Bake 15 minutes or until cake springs back when lightly touched.

2. In small saucepan over medium heat, melt remaining 1/4 cup butter; add remaining 1/4 cup cocoa and remaining Eagle Brand. Stir in powdered sugar and nuts. Spread on warm cake.   *Makes one 15×10-inch cake*

Mini Cheesecakes

1 1/2 cups graham cracker or chocolate wafer crumbs

1/4 cup sugar

1/4 cup (1/2 stick) butter or margarine, melted

3 (8-ounce) packages cream cheese, softened

1 (14-ounce) can EAGLE® BRAND Sweetened Condensed Milk
   (NOT evaporated milk)

3 eggs

2 teaspoons vanilla extract

1. Preheat oven to 300°F. Combine crumbs, sugar and butter; press equal portions onto bottoms of 24 lightly greased or paper-lined muffin cups.

2. In large mixing bowl, beat cream cheese until fluffy. Gradually beat in Eagle Brand until smooth. Add eggs and vanilla; mix well. Spoon equal amounts of mixture (about 3 tablespoons) into prepared cups. Bake 20 minutes or until cakes spring back when lightly touched. Cool.* Chill. Garnish as desired. Refrigerate leftovers.

Makes about 2 dozen mini cheesecakes

If greased muffin cups are used, cool baked cheesecakes. Freeze 15 minutes; remove with narrow spatula. Proceed as directed above.

Prep Time: 20 minutes
Bake Time: 20 minutes

Chocolate Mini Cheesecakes: Melt 1 cup (6 ounces) semi-sweet chocolate chips; mix into batter. Proceed as directed above, baking 20 to 25 minutes.

German Chocolate Cake

1 (18.25-ounce) package chocolate cake mix

1 cup water

3 eggs

1/2 cup vegetable oil

1 (14-ounce) can EAGLE® BRAND Sweetened Condensed Milk
    (NOT evaporated milk), divided

3 tablespoons butter or margarine

1 egg yolk

1/3 cup flaked coconut

1/3 cup chopped pecans

1 teaspoon vanilla extract

1. Preheat oven to 350°F. Grease and flour 13×9-inch baking pan. In large mixing bowl, combine cake mix, water, 3 eggs, oil and 1/3 cup Eagle Brand. Beat at low speed until moistened; beat at high speed 2 minutes.

2. Pour into prepared pan. Bake 40 to 45 minutes or until wooden pick inserted near center comes out clean.

3. In small saucepan over medium heat, combine remaining Eagle Brand, butter and egg yolk. Cook and stir until thickened, about 6 minutes. Add coconut, pecans and vanilla; spread over warm cake. Store covered in refrigerator. *Makes 10 to 12 servings*

Prep Time: 15 minutes
Bake Time: 40 to 45 minutes

German Chocolate Cake

Frozen Mocha Cheesecake

1 1/4 cups chocolate wafer cookie crumbs (about 24 wafers)

1/4 cup sugar

1/4 cup butter or margarine, melted

1 (8-ounce) package cream cheese, softened

1 (14-ounce) can EAGLE® BRAND Sweetened Condensed Milk
   (NOT evaporated milk)

2/3 cup chocolate-flavored syrup

1 to 2 tablespoons instant coffee

1 teaspoon hot water

1 cup (1/2 pint) whipping cream, whipped

Additional chocolate crumbs, if desired

1. In medium mixing bowl, combine crumbs, sugar and butter; press firmly on bottom and up side of 8- or 9-inch springform pan or 13×9-inch baking pan.

2. In large mixing bowl, beat cream cheese until fluffy. Gradually beat in Eagle Brand and chocolate syrup until smooth.

3. In small mixing bowl, dissolve coffee in water; add to cream cheese mixture. Mix well. Fold in whipped cream. Pour into crust; cover. Freeze 6 hours or overnight. Garnish with chocolate crumbs, if desired. Store leftovers in freezer.   *Makes one 8- or 9-inch cheesecake*

Chocolate Chip Cheesecake

1 1/2 cups finely crushed crème-filled chocolate sandwich cookie
        crumbs (about 18 cookies)
    2 to 3 tablespoons butter or margarine, melted
    3 (8-ounce) packages cream cheese, softened
    1 (14-ounce) can EAGLE® BRAND Sweetened Condensed Milk
        (NOT evaporated milk)
    3 eggs
    2 teaspoons vanilla extract
    1 cup mini semi-sweet chocolate chips, divided
    1 teaspoon all-purpose flour

1. Preheat oven to 300°F. In small mixing bowl, combine cookie crumbs and butter; press firmly on bottom of 9-inch springform pan.

2. In large mixing bowl, beat cream cheese until fluffy. Gradually beat in Eagle Brand until smooth. Add eggs and vanilla; mix well.

3. In small bowl, toss 1/2 cup chips with flour to coat; stir into cheese mixture. Pour into crust. Sprinkle remaining 1/2 cup chips evenly over top.

4. Bake 1 hour or until cake springs back when lightly touched. Cool to room temperature. Chill thoroughly. Garnish as desired. Refrigerate leftovers.   *Makes one 9-inch cheesecake*

Helpful Hint: For best distribution of chips throughout cheesecake, do not oversoften or overbeat cream cheese.

Holiday Cheese Tarts

1 (8-ounce) package cream cheese, softened
1 (14-ounce) can EAGLE® BRAND Sweetened Condensed Milk
(NOT evaporated milk)
⅓ cup lemon juice from concentrate
1 teaspoon vanilla extract
2 (4-ounce) packages single serve graham cracker crumb pie crusts
Assorted fruit (strawberries, blueberries, bananas, raspberries,
orange segments, cherries, kiwi fruit, grapes, pineapple, etc.)
¼ cup apple jelly, melted, if desired

1. In medium mixing bowl, beat cream cheese until fluffy. Gradually beat in Eagle Brand until smooth. Stir in lemon juice and vanilla.

2. Spoon into crusts. Chill 2 hours or until set. Just before serving, top with fruit; brush with jelly, if desired. Refrigerate leftovers.

Makes 12 tarts

Prep Time: 10 minutes
Chill Time: 2 hours

Holiday Cheese Tarts

Chocolate Almond Torte

4 eggs, separated

1/2 cup (1 stick) butter or margarine, softened

1 cup sugar

1 teaspoon almond extract

1 teaspoon vanilla extract

1 cup finely chopped toasted almonds

3/4 cup all-purpose flour

1/2 cup unsweetened cocoa

1/2 teaspoon baking powder

1/2 teaspoon baking soda

2/3 cup milk

Chocolate Almond Frosting (recipe follows)

1. Line 2 (8- or 9-inch) round cake pans with waxed paper. Preheat oven to 350°F. In small mixing bowl, beat egg whites until soft peaks form; set aside.

2. In large mixing bowl, beat butter and sugar until fluffy. Add egg yolks and extracts; mix well.

3. In medium mixing bowl, combine almonds, flour, cocoa, baking powder and baking soda; add alternately with milk to butter mixture, beating well after each addition.

4. Fold in beaten egg whites. Pour into prepared pans. Bake 18 to 20 minutes or until wooden pick inserted near centers comes out clean. Cool 10 minutes; remove from pans. Cool completely.

5. Prepare Chocolate Almond Frosting. Split each cake layer; fill and frost with frosting. Store covered in refrigerator.

Makes one 4-layer cake

Prep Time: 30 minutes
Bake Time: 18 to 20 minutes

Chocolate Almond Frosting

    2 (1-ounce) squares semi-sweet chocolate, chopped
    1 (14-ounce) can EAGLE® BRAND Sweetened Condensed Milk
        (NOT evaporated milk)
    1 teaspoon almond extract

1. In heavy saucepan over medium heat, melt chocolate with Eagle Brand. Cook and stir until mixture thickens, about 10 minutes.

2. Remove from heat; cool 10 minutes. Stir in almond extract; cool.

Makes about 1¹/₂ cups

Prep Time: 20 minutes

Cookies 'n' Crème Fudge

3 (6-ounce) packages white chocolate baking squares
1 (14-ounce) can EAGLE® BRAND Sweetened Condensed Milk
    (NOT evaporated milk)
$^1/_8$ teaspoon salt
2 cups coarsely crushed chocolate crème-filled sandwich cookies
    (about 20 cookies)

1. Line 8-inch square baking pan with foil. In heavy saucepan over low heat, melt chocolate with Eagle Brand and salt. Remove from heat. Stir in crushed cookies. Spread evenly in prepared pan. Chill 2 hours or until firm.

2. Turn fudge onto cutting board. Peel off foil; cut into squares. Store tightly covered at room temperature.   *Makes about 2 1/2 pounds*

Prep Time: 10 minutes
Chill Time: 2 hours

Chocolate Raspberry Truffles

1 (14-ounce) can EAGLE® BRAND Sweetened Condensed Milk
    (NOT evaporated milk)
1/4 cup raspberry liqueur
2 tablespoons butter or margarine
2 tablespoons seedless raspberry jam
2 (12-ounce) packages semi-sweet chocolate chips
1/2 cup powdered sugar or ground toasted almonds

1. In large microwave-safe bowl, combine first 4 ingredients. Microwave at HIGH (100% power) 3 minutes.

2. Stir in chips until smooth. Cover and chill 1 hour.

3. Shape mixture into 1-inch balls and roll in powdered sugar or almonds. Store covered at room temperature. *Makes 4 dozen truffles*

Prep Time: 10 minutes
Cook Time: 3 minutes
Chill Time: 1 hour

INDEX

VOLUME MEASUREMENTS (dry)

$1/8$ teaspoon = 0.5 mL
$1/4$ teaspoon = 1 mL
$1/2$ teaspoon = 2 mL
$3/4$ teaspoon = 4 mL
1 teaspoon = 5 mL
1 tablespoon = 15 mL
2 tablespoons = 30 mL
$1/4$ cup = 60 mL
$1/3$ cup = 75 mL
$1/2$ cup = 125 mL
$2/3$ cup = 150 mL
$3/4$ cup = 175 mL
1 cup = 250 mL
2 cups = 1 pint = 500 mL
3 cups = 750 mL
4 cups = 1 quart = 1 L

VOLUME MEASUREMENTS (fluid)

1 fluid ounce (2 tablespoons) = 30 mL
4 fluid ounces ($1/2$ cup) = 125 mL
8 fluid ounces (1 cup) = 250 mL
12 fluid ounces ($1 1/2$ cups) = 375 mL
16 fluid ounces (2 cups) = 500 mL

WEIGHTS (mass)

$1/2$ ounce = 15 g
1 ounce = 30 g
3 ounces = 90 g
4 ounces = 120 g
8 ounces = 225 g
10 ounces = 285 g
12 ounces = 360 g
16 ounces = 1 pound = 450 g

DIMENSIONS

$1/16$ inch = 2 mm
$1/8$ inch = 3 mm
$1/4$ inch = 6 mm
$1/2$ inch = 1.5 cm
$3/4$ inch = 2 cm
1 inch = 2.5 cm

OVEN TEMPERATURES

250°F = 120°C
275°F = 140°C
300°F = 150°C
325°F = 160°C
350°F = 180°C
375°F = 190°C
400°F = 200°C
425°F = 220°C
450°F = 230°C

BAKING PAN SIZES

Utensil	Size in Inches/Quarts	Metric Volume	Size in Centimeters
Baking or	$8 \times 8 \times 2$	2 L	$20 \times 20 \times 5$
Cake Pan	$9 \times 9 \times 2$	2.5 L	$23 \times 23 \times 5$
(square or	$12 \times 8 \times 2$	3 L	$30 \times 20 \times 5$
rectangular)	$13 \times 9 \times 2$	3.5 L	$33 \times 23 \times 5$
Loaf Pan	$8 \times 4 \times 3$	1.5 L	$20 \times 10 \times 7$
	$9 \times 5 \times 3$	2 L	$23 \times 13 \times 7$
Round Layer	$8 \times 1 1/2$	1.2 L	20×4
Cake Pan	$9 \times 1 1/2$	1.5 L	23×4
Pie Plate	$8 \times 1 1/4$	750 mL	20×3
	$9 \times 1 1/4$	1 L	23×3
Baking Dish	1 quart	1 L	—
or Casserole	$1 1/2$ quart	1.5 L	—
	2 quart	2 L	—